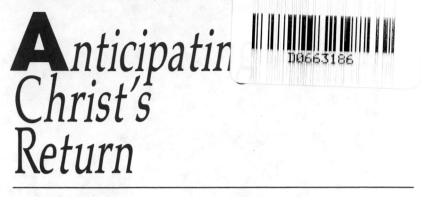

Anticipating Christ's Return

Stephen D. & Jacalyn Eyre

A Month
of
Guided
Quiet
Times
in
Revelation

INTERVARSITY PRESS
DOWNERS GROVE, ILLINOIS 60515

InterVarsity Press® is the book-publishing division of InterVarsity Christian Fellowship®, a student move-ment active on campus at hundreds of universities, colleges and schools of nursing in the United States of America, and a member movement of the International Fellowship of Evangelical Students. For information about local and regional activities, write Public Relations Dept., InterVarsity Christian Fellowship, 6400 Schroeder Rd., P.O. Box 7895, Madison, WI 53707-7895.

Cover photograph: Robert Flesher

ISBN 0-8308-1182-6

Printed in the United States of America ∞

15	14	13	12	11	10	9	8	7	6	5	4	3	2	1
04	03	02	01	00	99	98	97	96	95	94				

Introducing *Anticipating Christ's Return*

The book of Revelation is a strange book full of images that include plagues of boils, beings with eyes all over their bodies, angels and demons, dragons and beasts, lakes of fire, and lots of other unusual things. Some Christians avoid Revelation altogether. It's too weird. Others become obsessed by it. Convinced they have discovered a secret key to unlock its strange meanings, they plot the coming events of world history.

Around the time of my (Steve's) conversion, the pastor of our church was doing a series on the book of Revelation. The characters in Revelation such as the beast and the false prophet were matched to public personalities of the day, while nations such as Gog and Magog were all tied to current international events. It was exhilarating to think I had become a believer in the last days.

But not everything turned out the way it was supposed to. Those personalities who had been labeled as the beast and false prophet all left political office. The international scene changed. The nations that were supposedly mentioned in the book of Revelation ceased to exist. It's now over twenty-five years since those thrilling sermons, and we are all still here.

For a while after that, I lost interest in the book of Revelation. What drew me back was an underlying tension I discovered in the teachings of Jesus and the New Testament. I found that I needed the book of Revelation to make sense of everything else I read.

The Promised Kingdom

The disciples felt the tension I am speaking of. Just before Jesus ascended to heaven, they asked, "Are you at this time going to restore the kingdom to Israel?" They were trying to put together some pieces that didn't quite seem to fit. What I believe they were asking is, "Is it time yet to complete what you came to do? You preached that the kingdom of God was at hand. Under your ministry the blind received sight, the lame walked, those with leprosy were cured, the deaf heard, the dead were raised and the poor had the good news preached to them." I too want to ask the Lord, "When are you going to finish what you started?"

There are those who say that the ministry of Jesus is continuing in the ministry of the church. To some extent I think they are right. We preach about Jesus, and people get saved. I believe as well that people get healed today, both through answered prayer and through perhaps more spectacular means of people with the gift of healing. And that's great. But it is still incomplete.

If I understand Jesus' message, he promised a new order or reality in which his miracles were only hints or tokens of what was to come. When he proclaimed, "The kingdom of God is at hand," he was proclaiming a new order of life in which the meek would inherit the earth, where the lion would lie down with the lamb and in which the source of pain and weeping would be abolished forever. Answers to prayer and miracles of all kinds are nice, but they don't fix the world. People who get healed from one disease still get sick from something else, and they, along with all of us, die. There must be something more.

Certainly Mary expected something more from her son. In speaking with her relative Elizabeth about the child in her own womb, Mary exults because through the child God "has scattered those who are proud in their inmost thoughts. He has brought down rulers from their thrones but has lifted up the humble. He has filled the hungry with good things but has sent the rich away empty" (Lk 1:51-53).

I bear the fruit of the Spirit, and I see the power of God at work in my ministry. But I find that something is not right inside me. Decisions made with what I thought were the best of intentions turn out to be self-centered and sinful. I find that my love for others tends to come with strings attached. I know the words of the apostle Paul, "For in my inner being I delight in God's law; but I see another law at work in the members of my body, waging war against the law of my mind and making me a prisoner of the law of sin at work within my members" (Rom 7:22-23).

With the disciples I want to know when Jesus is going to complete what he promised. When is the world going to be fixed? When am I going to be fixed?

In answer to my urgent questions the Lord has given me the wonderful book of Revelation. When I read Revelation now, I don't find detailed descriptions of the unfolding of world history by which I can interpret present events. What I do discover is that Jesus tells me that he is coming back to complete what he began. He shows me what the world will be like one day as he brings in the new heaven and earth. He assures me that the curse will be removed, that he will remove all suffering and every cause of pain. He shows that evil will be banished, sin judged, and everything he promised in his ministry will indeed come to pass.

In the meantime, I am supposed to live in tension. I am right to be frustrated as I struggle with God's new life inside of me and the remnants of sin that battle to control the members of my body. The very tension is a sign of life and hope.

Studying Revelation
I invite you to join us in a month of guided quiet times in the book of Revelation. As you read and pray through the passages, we believe that you will find your hope enhanced along with your tension. As you read Jesus' word to the seven churches in Asia, you will be challenged to a

deeper love and more consistent obedience. After Jesus' letter to the churches, we will jump past chapters 4—18. It's not because they aren't important, but because we couldn't cover the whole of Revelation in this guide. In the concluding chapters you will see that all Jesus' promises will be fulfilled in the coming new order of reality in the New Jerusalem.

There are several different ways to interpret Revelation. As we deal with controversial passages, we seek to ask the questions in a way that allows you to make some choices. However, whichever choice you make, there can be a common ground in eager anticipation of Jesus' return.

The central theme running through the book is that Jesus is coming back soon. In my studies of the Bible I've come to appreciate the sense of throbbing anticipation that my pastor of twenty-five years ago created in me. I was sure that Jesus was coming back any day. As I read Jesus' instruction to the disciples in the book of Revelation, I believe that he wants us to live with just that sense of anticipation. It is our hope that your time in these guided quiet times will create that same sense of anticipation in you.

Using the Guide

The format for each day includes five elements.

Introduction: This is brief, a couple of paragraphs that allow us to set the tone and introduce the issues for your quiet time.

Approach: This is designed to help you deal with mental and emotional obstacles that we all struggle with as we seek to shift our attention from ourselves to God and his Word. Take some time with the approach question, five minutes or more. Use it to reach out to God so that you know you are meeting with him as you begin your study of his Word.

Study: These questions are written to help you focus on the content of the passage. The questions focus on the essential issues of each passage and on what they mean.

The New International Version is the translation we used to write the Spiritual Encounter Guide study questions. You can use another version, of course, but you will need to make adjustments as some of the questions may not make sense. Why the NIV? We think it is a good contemporary translation that brings out the meaning of the original texts.

Reflect: In this section, we use the spiritual tools of silence and imagination to help you apply the passage to your soul and life issues. As with the approach question, the more time you take with these questions, the more likely you will be to come away from your quiet time with a sense of personal encounter.

Pray: We offer a couple of suggestions for prayer. We expect that during this time you will develop your own prayer list as well. Take time to ask God for help and wisdom for yourself, your family, church, friends and whatever else you can think of.

Each quiet time will take you a minimum of twenty to thirty minutes, although you could easily spend more time if you work through the questions in a leisurely, reflective manner.

Writing this guide was a team effort. In the introductions you'll read stories from Steve's experience, and in the study sections you'll see more of Jackie's hand.

How to Think About Quiet Time

Some people think of a quiet time as Bible study and prayer. We think of a quiet time as an encounter with God in which you do Bible study and pray.

The difference between the two definitions may seem small, but we think it is crucial. If a quiet time is just Bible study and prayer, then the relational dimension may easily get lost. You may end up merely going through the motions of religious activities and gaining some new information. However, if your goal is to set aside time to meet with God, then the whole dynamic of the quiet time is changed. It becomes a cultivation of a relationship. It becomes an opportunity for discipleship as the Lord himself meets with us.

Of course, because God's Word is his means of instructing us, we can't

expect to learn from him unless we are spending serious time consider-
ing what has been written down for us. Likewise, prayer is the means
by which we talk with him and ask for his help. But we must be careful
that prayer involves listening as well as asking. If we allow our prayer
to degenerate into offering God a list of our wants and recommendations
for running the world, then we are no longer in a personal teacher-stu-
dent relationship.

A word of caution: this guide is not intended to be used legalistically.

It's funny thing, but in my experience, people who don't have quiet times
don't feel much guilt about it. On the other hand, people who think that
quiet times are important experience a good deal of guilt. It seems that the
expectation is that you must have one every day or else be a spiritual failure.
Quiet time guides can nourish this inclination, because it is obvious when
it has been a couple of days since you last used the guide. Of course, this
guilt feeds on itself, and after a while you avoid the guide altogether because
you don't want to confront your sense of failure.

We like the advice that Brother Lawrence gave in *Practicing the
Presence of God*. He wrote that he never condemned himself for missing
the mark in his times with God. He knew that God was not surprised at
his "failure." He knew that God was delighted whenever he took the
time to pray and was not a petulant, condemning father when he didn't.
If you follow his example, you too will find that you meet with God not
because you have to but because you desire to.

In order to keep the guide from being a "guilt producer," we have not
divided it by weeks. Instead, we have merely numbered the studies one
through twenty-five. Some weeks you may have a quiet time six out of
seven days. Other weeks you may only have one or two. God doesn't
love you any more on the weeks when you have a quiet time every day
or less on the weeks when you have no quiet time at all.

Living in Hope
There is another tension that we hope you will experience as you move

through these guided quiet times. We want you to be nourished by the Lord's presence in his Word. At the same time we hope that you experience a yearning hunger for his return. Jesus wants us to live on the razor edge of expectation:

No one knows about that day or hour, not even the angels in heaven, nor the Son, but only the Father. . . . Therefore keep watch, because you do not know on what day your Lord will come. . . . So you also must be ready, because the Son of Man will come at an hour when you do not expect him. (Mt 24:36, 42, 44)

Day 1
The Revelation of Jesus Christ
Revelation 1:1-3

Graham, a friend of ours in England, tells stories about his colorful grandfather and the Bible. On occasion he would gather a crowd by pointing to a piece of cloth he dropped on the sidewalk and shouting, "It's alive!" When people came running to see what he was pointing to, he would lift up the cloth to reveal a Bible. Taking up the Bible and waving it in the air above his head, he would begin to preach to his listeners about the virtues of the Bible.

The Bible is alive. Something happens when you read it. The words on the page are more than nice ideas or guidelines for moral behavior. It's more than a theology textbook. Something reaches up from the page to address the mind and the heart. Something or Someone comes through the words to call and challenge, to provoke, stimulate and entice. It is similar to what the two disciples on the road to Emmaus experienced on the resurrection day after they met the Lord: "Were not our hearts burning within us while he talked with us on the road and opened the Scriptures to us?" (Lk 24:32).

As you read the book of Revelation, it is possible that you may enter into the same experience as the disciples on the road to Emmaus. The One who spoke the book to John may, if you ask him, lift the words from the page and speak them to you. When that happens, the words will feed your soul, shape your thoughts and strengthen your heart.

Approach

In Revelation 1:3 a blessing is offered to those who read, hear and take to heart the book of Revelation. Plan to read each day's passage silently, then out loud, and determine to think about it during your day. Read Revelation 1:3 out loud now, and write a prayer asking the Lord to allow you to take it to heart.

Study

1. Read Revelation 1:1-3. What various means is God using to make known the message of the revelation?

2. Who are the people involved in sending and receiving the revelation?

3. What assurance are we given that the messages about the future are trustworthy?

4. The revelation is about "what must soon take place." There are a number of different ways to interpret this. Commentators have different opinions. What do you think? Does Revelation deal with events

| in the first century when the words were first spoken? | throughout the unfolding history of the church? | at the end of time? | including all the preceding? |

Reflect

1. The word *revelation* means "uncovering." The book of Revelation is not merely about the future in general, but about the revealing of Jesus Christ. Imagine that there is a veil across your heart. Ask the Lord to remove it so that you may see his presence in your life. Sit for a while and allow him to work. Write down your impressions and emotions.

2. The time frame of Revelation is the impending future. Jesus wants us to know what is going to happen so we can live and think accordingly. How would your behavior be affected if you knew what Jesus was going to do in your life within the next week or so? In your reflection take into account your work, your family, your friends, your time and your money.

Pray

Ask the Lord to come back soon.

Ask the Lord to give a sense of anticipation for his return.

Pray for several other believers, that they would grow in a love for God's Word.

Day 2
The Coming of Christ
Revelation 1:4-8

Want to paralyze your mind? Nothing will do it quicker than a child's questions about spiritual issues. These sorts of questions come up when you are sitting on the edge of the bed at night, ready to give a final kiss goodnight and say prayers.

Do animals have souls?

Why did God make mosquitoes? (Or, Why does God let bad things happen to good people?)

Why did God let my grandmother die?

Where did God come from?

Some of these questions are amusing, some are painful. For all my reading and theological training, I can't answer them.

The last one, "Where did God come from?" is one that sent me spinning as a child. It still does. To the human mind, everything has a beginning. People are born and die. Projects are started and finished. Even the universe, however far back we go, four or even six billion years ago, still had a beginning. And in the other direction, although it is a long way off, physicists can calculate that eventually the stars will use up their finite source of energy, burn out and grow cold.

Yet for God there is no beginning. Nor is there an end. He just is. When Moses asked God for his name, the answer came: "I AM WHO I AM." God just is. As Jesus sends his words of greeting to seven of churches in Asia, he reveals himself as "the one who is, and who was, and who is to come." Although we can't understand it, it is that assurance that makes both the book of Revelation and the whole Bible live from one generation to the next. It was true for those who first heard it, and it is true for you as well.

Approach

There are many things we can know about God, but much that we can't. Get quiet and listen. What feelings come as you pause to consider the mystery and majesty of God?

Study

1. Read Revelation 1:4-8. This is the revelation of Jesus Christ. What are we told about him in these verses?

2. The Father is described as the alpha and omega (the first and last letters of the Greek alphabet) and as the one "who is, and who was, and who is to come." What does this reveal about God?

3. According to these verses, why would some people be anticipating the return of Christ and others be terrified by it?

4. Jesus makes his people a kingdom and priests to his God. (This is a direct reference to Exodus 19:5-6 and God's purpose for Israel after he delivered them from the bondage of Egypt.) What does this suggest for the role of God's people in the world?

5. The image of Christ's return in the clouds is taken from Daniel 7:13-14. Read those verses and compare them with today's verses. What do they tell about Jesus Christ?

Reflect
1. See if you can glimpse in your mind's eye the majestic image of Christ returning in the clouds. How do you respond?

2. Jesus is the ultimate ruler of the nations. Behind all the political maneuvering, Jesus Christ is working out his will for the world. Get a newspaper or think about current national and world news. List the issues and events in the space below and then acknowledge that Jesus is Lord over all that happens.

3. John records that Jesus has freed us from our sins by his blood. Sit back and get quiet. Picture him washing your heart from all your sins. Rest for a while and allow yourself to enjoy being clean before God. After you have done so, write down your impressions.

Pray
Ask the Lord to show himself to several of your friends who don't know him as the Lord who died for them.

Pray that your church might be a witness to the saving work of God in this world.

Day 3
The Appearance of Christ
Revelation 1:9-16

S ome Christians imply—and I have been guilty of this in my own evangelistic zeal—that when you accept Jesus as your Lord, life gets better and things get easier. That, however, has not been my experience. Life was hard before I gave my life to Christ, and it is still hard. Yet something is different when we believe. The struggles don't go away, but they become meaningful. We know that the pains of life are servants of the Lord to work his will in us and through us. At least they are supposed to be.

I am struggling with some pains of the past as they are reflected in my family life and ministry. I am tired of the issues and it's not really the first time that I have faced them. But each time I "solve them," a few years later they come back with a new twist. When I ask the Lord for help, I don't get a program for self-improvement and happiness. He does not "fix" me. What happens is that I get a new glimpse of him. As I am forced beyond myself to reach up in aching prayer, I sense his presence, understand his character and rely on his power in ways that I didn't before.

John is in a hard situation as he writes Revelation. He is a prisoner of the Romans, exiled to a small island, cut off from fellow believers. While John is there, the Lord comes to him with an awesome unveiling of his presence. What he saw will, even for you and me today, transform the most difficult problem from a life-destroying threat to a life-giving opportunity for faith. In all struggles we need to be reminded that we don't need solutions; we need the Lord. If we are open, he will show us just what we need to know about him to keep going and growing.

Approach
The Lord is always making himself known to us. Perhaps not in the same graphic way that John experienced, but he is showing himself nevertheless. Make a list of your struggles and hurts. Give them over to him and then sit quietly, looking for him to come to you with his nourishing presence.

Study
1. Read Revelation 1:9-16. John is a prisoner on the desolate island of Patmos. What does this passage suggest about John's attitude when the revelation was given to him (vv. 10-11)?

2. The description of Jesus is full of symbolism. Here is my suggestion

of the meaning of each of the images that depict Jesus:

Image	Meaning
golden sash across chest	royalty
lampstands among which Jesus stands	the churches
white head and hair	maturity and wisdom
blazing eyes	penetrating knowledge
voice of rushing waters	majestic power
seven stars in right hand	message of the churches
sharp sword from mouth	Word of God
shining face like the sun	glory of God

How do you respond as you read John's description of the revelation of Jesus?

3. How would this vision of Jesus be an encouragement to John and to Christians in similar situations?

Reflect

1. John's attitude toward his exile on Patmos seems to be one of willing acceptance. When have you experienced struggles and/or resistance for your faith in Jesus Christ?

2. Jesus said that all of us would experience tribulation and struggle in this world. What is your response when you experience pain and suffering?

3. John's ability to have patient endurance comes from his sense of Christ's lordship and spiritual worship. Give your circumstances over to God. Worship him using the images in today's verses. Do your best to picture these images and to praise him for the truths about him that they convey.

Pray

The revelation is given through John to the churches of Asia. Pray today for churches around the world, that they would be open to hear what the Lord has to say to them.

Pray for strength and boldness to share your faith in Jesus Christ with others who don't yet believe.

Day 4
The Message of Christ
Revelation 1:17-20

Someone once commented, "Jesus came and preached the kingdom of God. It was wonderful. The lame were healed, the blind got their sight, and the hungry were fed. After he left, all we were left with was the church . . . what happened?"

Let's be honest. The church has a mixed track record, and its reputation is tarnished. Consider the Crusades in the twelfth and thirteenth centuries, the Inquisition in the fifteenth and sixteenth centuries, the condemnation of Galileo in the seventeenth century, the support of slavery in the nineteenth century, the fund-raising antics of media evangelists in the twentieth century . . . the list, I suppose, could go on for pages.

The resurrected Lord himself has a few concerns about his church. That is why he chose to speak the book of Revelation through John. He wants the seven churches of Asia to know what he thinks about them. With a couple of exceptions, he wants the churches to clean up their act.

There are problems in the churches that are dangerous and could destroy their mission and ministry.

Keep in mind, however, that even with all the problems, Jesus Christ loves his church. He sends these messages to the churches precisely because he values them so highly. They are integral to his plan. Flawed as it is this side of heaven, his church is the means by which he is bringing his kingdom from heaven to the earth.

In the next seven quiet times, we will look at Jesus' letter to each of the churches. There are several things to keep in mind as we do. The first is the importance of the church. Jesus loves his church. The second thing is that Jesus reveals something unique about himself to each church, which is just what they need to know to be put back on the right track. The third is that Jesus' message to the *seven* churches has an application to *all* the churches through the march of history. The number seven is the clue. In Scripture it means completion, fullness—the big picture. That means that each day you can find out something about the church that will help you and the church you belong to.

Approach
Seeing more about Jesus is always the first and best answer to all our problems. One of the best ways to open our spiritual eyes is to cultivate a thankful heart. Sit for a while in quiet. Make a list of things that you are thankful for till you can see from your heart how good Jesus is.

Study
1. Read Revelation 1:17-20. How does Jesus' description of himself to John bring together the characteristics of the Father and the Son mentioned in verses 4-6?

2. Jesus wants John to know about his power over death:

Symbol	Meaning
first and last	the source and the consummation of life
living one	the eternal Person
dead and now alive forever	the One who has experienced and conquered death
holder of the keys of death and Hades	the One with authority over death

How would this give John comfort in the experience of his shock of seeing the risen Lord Jesus and the pain of his circumstances?

3. The stars and the lampstand are symbols of the church and its message. What is the nature of the message the churches are about to receive?

Reflect

1. Jesus is the Lord of life and the conqueror of death. When have you experienced a fear of death? What were the circumstances, and how were you affected?

What hope does this picture of Jesus give as you face your future?

2. The churches of Jesus Christ are pictured as lights on a lampstand. How has God used the church as a means of light in your own life?

3. What differences would there be in your life if you were not part of a fellowship of believers?

Pray
Pray for the church, that it would hold forth the light of Jesus Christ for the world.

Pray that the Lord would show himself in new ways to you and your Christian friends.

Day 5

Ephesus: *Love Me*
Revelation 2:1-7

I was clobbered by the Lord a couple of weeks ago, and I am still feeling the effects.

About ten years ago I came to the conclusion that I needed, and that most Christians need, regular extended times of personal worship. I got a copy of Richard Foster's book *The Celebration of Discipline* and set about using it as a manual. I read it over and over, especially the chapters on silence and solitude, prayer and meditation. From there I branched out on my own to Bernard of Clairvaux, Thomas à Kempis, Augustine, the sayings of the Desert Fathers, the Conferences of Cassian and a host of others.

Shortly after I started spending extended times in prayer, I ran into suppressed pain and sublimated fears in the depths of my heart. Facing those was a messy, dark time, but God took me through it. And something wonderful happened. I began to sense the presence of the Lord in ways I had only heard about. Whenever I sat down to pray, the room frequently filled up with a rich, full, tender silence. God was there. My heart was drawn into peace, praise and adoration.

In the last couple of years, those extended times became mostly a memory. Occasionally I took a quiet day or spend a couple of hours in silence, but not often. Instead my life was filled with planning meetings, preparing talks, leading Bible discussions and orchestrating worship services. Prayers were short times of hurried business as I asked God to fix this or straighten out that. God was answering my spoken and unspoken prayers in wonderful ways. More people in my church were studying the Bible, sharing their faith and seeking out spiritual help than ever before.

Yet while God was blessing my ministry, I don't believe that he was pleased with me. He doesn't merely want my ministry efforts, he wants my love. He wants me. So, as is his way with his loved ones who continually resist, he allowed a large dose of pain to strike my heart and arrest my pace. I hurt so much that the only thing I could do was cry out for help—a long, fervent cry. His warm, loving response was "Welcome back, son. I love you."

As you read about Jesus' letter to the church of Ephesus, you will see that after two thousand years neither the Lord nor his church has changed. We put other things in his place, and he in his love calls us to come back.

Approach
Desire for God should motivate us. Sit back, put this book down, and close your eyes. Enjoy being with God. Take five minutes or more and sit in his presence. Don't force your feelings, but see if affection for him will rise up in your heart. Before you move on to the study, make a few notes about your responses and perceptions.

Study

1. Read Revelation 2:1-7. Fill in the chart with Jesus' message to the Ephesian church.

Description of Jesus	
Commendation	
Warning	
Command	
Reward	

2. How would you characterize the Ephesian church?

3. How does Jesus' description of himself relate to his warning?

4. What must the Ephesians overcome to receive Jesus' reward?

Reflect

1. The Ephesians are commended for their hard work and their defense of orthodoxy. What do you think the Lord would commend your church for?

2. No one is sure who the Nicolaitans are, but apparently they were false teachers that the Ephesians were on guard against. What false teachings do you think the church needs to stand against today?

3. With all their good characteristics, the Ephesians were working hard in a cold orthodoxy rather than in a warm love of the Lord. How would you describe the state of your love of Jesus Christ?

4. Picture yourself standing before Jesus as he described himself to the Ephesians. Ask the Lord what he likes about you. Sit quietly for a while in a listening silence and then write down your impressions and perceptions.

Pray
Ask the Lord to bring back your "first love."

Pray that your church would be faithful in standing for the truth of Jesus Christ.

Day 6
Smyrna: Be Brave
Revelation 2:8-11

I can't figure the Lord out.

All power in heaven and on earth belongs to Jesus, right? Isn't it so that Jesus loves his people and has all that power available to help us? Then it follows, does it not, that he would naturally remove all sources of pain and suffering?

But it doesn't seem to work that way. Early Christians got thrown to the lions or used as torches in Nero's gardens. Christians today lose their jobs, die from cancer or other diseases, experience divorce and, in general, suffer the ills of this world. I want to ask God, What is going on?

The Lord's response to the church in Smyrna is his response to me. Evidently, he doesn't feel that he must deliver me from pain and persecution. As I struggle, I must keep in mind that I don't have all the facts and don't see the whole picture. What appears to be a desperate situation to me may not be from his perspective. What appears to be poverty may in fact be untold wealth. And as for death, the ultimate fear, despite what it looks like, it is not the end.

Actually, it's not merely that I can't figure him out, but that I don't like the way he makes life work. I don't want to die, get sick, be belittled or persecuted by others. His response is, as you will see in your quiet time today, "Son, you will just have to trust me."

Approach

Consider: what questions do you have for God, and why are those issues important to you? Write out your questions and tell him your concerns. Once you have done that, get quiet and listen.

Study

1. Read Revelation 2:8-11. Fill in the chart with Jesus' message to the church in Smyrna.

Description of Jesus	
Commendation	
Warning	
Command	
Reward	

2. From Jesus' words to the church at Smyrna, what would you say were their earthly prospects?

3. How would Jesus' description of himself provide comfort and strength?

Reflect

1. Satan tests believers, and the Lord allows it. In what ways has the Lord allowed you to be tested?

What was painful about it?

What difference did it make in you?

2. It appears that Jesus is going to allow some members of the church in Smyrna to die for their faith in him. How do you respond to that?

3. Jesus offers comfort not by removal of pain but by knowledge of what is to come after death. Picture yourself on the other side of death, free from your current struggles. After sitting with the Lord in his presence for a while, write down how such a perspective makes a difference in the way you respond to the trials of today.

Pray
Ask God to increase your faith in his victory over death.
    Pray for Christians who are suffering for their faith.

Day 7
Pergamum: Be Pure
Revelation 2:12-17

I am up for spiritual adventures. Several years ago one of my friends accused me of dwelling on the edges of orthodoxy. I was hurt . . . and delighted. I am as orthodox as can be. I believe the Apostles' Creed, the Nicene Creed and the Westminster Confession with all my heart. (Well, there are one or two things about the Westminster Confession I would be willing to discuss.) I believe that the Bible is God's true, inspired and trustworthy Word that is all-sufficient to feed faith and instruct my mind.

On the other hand, I want to know how it all applies today. I don't want to just read about what God did two thousand years ago; I want to participate with him in the adventure of life. I don't want to just read about what God said to other people; I want him to speak to me. I don't want just to hear other people talk about the power of prayer; I want to pray and see things happen. If that puts me on the fringes of orthodoxy, then that's where you will find me. Frankly, I prefer to think of it as being on the front line, the cutting edge.

Ah, but there is danger out here. Sometimes the lines get blurred. Is

God speaking to me, or is it just that I am listening to my own thoughts and attributing them to God? Did God call me to my latest project, or is that merely my need to be busy, successful and productive? Sometimes such questions only become clear after I have made a wrong decision and have to face the consequences.

God has made provision for people like me. It's called the gift of repentance. Rather than condemnation, repentance is the Lord's means of getting me back inside the lines and on the narrow road. He simply calls me to stop and turn around. It is no fun, but I wouldn't have it any other way. It gives me the courage to follow him with zest.

Approach

When we repent, we are freed from our various kinds of slavery and liberated to have Jesus as the center of our hearts. What things, people, actions, projects may be leading you down the wrong road? Make a list. Once you have done so, picture yourself giving it over to him. Sit for a while in worship. Make a few notes about your impressions and emotional responses.

Study

1. Read Revelation 2:12-17. Fill in the chart with Jesus' message to the church of Pergamum.

Description of Jesus	
Commendation	
Warning	
Command	
Reward	

2. The Christians at Pergamum have a firm faith but are overly tolerant of error. What do you think is wrong with eating food sacrificed to idols?

3. How is the Pergamum church similar to the Smyrna church in its problems and different from the Ephesus church in its weaknesses?

4. The sword from Jesus' mouth is the Word of God. How will it address the problems of the Pergamum church?

Reflect
1. Balaam (Num 22-24) showed any enemy of Israel how to entice the Israelites to sin. In what ways do you think that Christians today are allowing ungodly practices and ideas into the church?

How do you feel the effects of the world's pressure on your life?

2. Christ promises divine food (hidden manna) in place of food sacrificed

to idols. What do you think the Lord offers you in place of temptations that you struggle with?

3. David, in Psalm 23, wrote that the Lord prepared a table for him in the presence of his enemies. Picture yourself in the Lord's presence, perhaps sitting by a table near a small stream. As you sit there, allow the Lord to give you food that nourishes and satisfies your soul. After a period of rest and quiet with him, write down your thoughts and impressions.

Pray
Ask the Lord to allow the church to repent from its worldliness.

Ask God to give you an appetite for him that won't be satisfied by anything else.

Day 8
Thyatira: Hate Idolatry
Revelation 2:18-29

*T*here is a church in our denomination that wants to ordain practicing homosexuals. Many of us are not happy about this and are doing what we can to prevent it. What we hear in response is that Christians are uptight about sexuality. God condemns all sin, so why is it that we seem to get hung up on sexual immorality?

One of the favorite means of idolatry in the Old Testament was the worship of the gods and goddesses by means of sexual intercourse. Temple prostitutes welcomed worshipers into their eager embrace. The religion was so widespread and developed that there was even neighborhood delivery available to those who didn't want to travel all the way to the main temple. The prophets of Israel condemned wandering after such gods and goddesses, calling it spiritual adultery.

The idolatrous sexuality of the Old Testament and the pagan world surfaced in the first churches of the New Testament. And it is surfacing today. In one sense, those who object to the church's moral code on sexuality are right: orthodox Christians do make a big deal about sex. But that is not because it is so bad, but because it is so powerful. It is a means by which we can be drawn away from God into the worship of others. Jesus won't tolerate that.

Approach

God loves you. He wants you to know it. He wants you to believe it. And he wants you to feel it. Invite God to embrace you, body and soul. How do you respond to his love? Write down your observations and impressions.

Study

1. Read Revelation 2:18-29. Fill in the chart with Jesus' message to the church of Thyatira.

Description of Jesus	
Commendation	
Warning	
Command	
Reward	

2. How might Jesus' detailed description of his judgment of the false teacher help the church correct the problem (vv. 22-23)?

Reflect

1. Jesus tells the Christians in Thyatira to hang on. The pressures of the world, Satan and our sin continually pull us away from God. How would you evaluate your sense of closeness to the Lord now as opposed to a year ago?

Distant   Intimate

What events and influences have contributed to your spiritual condition?

2. Jesus looks into the churches to discern their spiritual condition. He also looks into the mind and heart of each Christian. Open your heart up to the Lord, and ask him to search you and purify you. As you become aware of spiritual impurities, ask the Lord to cleanse you. Sit for a while in quiet and write down your thoughts and impressions.

Pray

Ask that your church would resist the seduction of false doctrine.

Pray for several of your fellow Christians. Ask that they would be empowered to hold on to their relationship with the Lord rather than slipping backwards.

Day 9
Sardis: Wake Up!
Revelation 3:1-6

I couldn't put my finger on it, but when I walked into the sanctuary of that church on Friday, there was a dullness about it, a spirit of slumber.

There was no visible reason for me to feel that way. It was a bright, open room decorated in white and green. The room was empty, so I wasn't responding to anyone else. Since I was exploring a pastoral position at the church, I returned Sunday morning to share in the leadership of the worship services. Sure enough, the singing was plodding and listless. The person who read the Scripture seemed bored. It was awful. I wanted to walk down the steps on the chancel and shout "Wake up!"

Someone once said that the spiritual awareness of the average Christian today is comparable to that of a small-town businessman at about two o'clock in the afternoon on a hot summer day after a big lunch. Many of us are drowsy and ready to drop off for a nice nap.

In our secular and materialistic culture we are not sure what spiritual life really is. Enchanted by two hundred years of modernity, we have moved God from the center of our culture to the edges. The message is, God is not really necessary for life, but it's OK if you believe in him as long as you don't go overboard. As the church carries on in such a culture, we are enticed into keeping the outward form of faith while losing touch with its vitality and reality.

Jesus' message to the church at Sardis calls us to shake off the spirit of slumber.

Approach
Sometimes it's hard to center on the Lord because there are so many distracting thoughts colliding in our minds. As you get quiet and focus on him, write down those distracting thoughts. After you have allowed yourself enough time to get them down on paper, hand them over to the Lord and ask him to free you to be with him.

Study
1. Read Revelation 3:1-6. Fill in the chart with Jesus' message to the church of Sardis.

Description of Jesus	
Commendation	
Warning	
Command	
Reward	

2. Jesus is portrayed as the one who holds the power of witness and mission in the churches. What do you think that the mission and witness of this church might have been like?

3. This church is not in good shape. How do you think Jesus' threat that he will come unexpectedly may help them?

4. Jesus says that he has not found their deeds complete in the sight of God. Based on what Jesus has said to the other churches, what might they need to do to make their deeds complete?

5. There are a few people in Sardis who have been faithful to the Lord. How would Jesus' assurances be important in light of the state of their church?

Reflect
1. Jesus calls the church at Sardis to wake up. Evidently, they were not aware of their spiritual condition. How would you describe the spiritual condition of your church? Mark it on the chart below.

Dead   Sleepy   Moderate   Waking Up   Alive

2. What events, issues and people are shaping the current spiritual condition of your church?

3. Jesus speaks not only to the church but to individual members. How would you describe your spiritual condition? Mark it on the chart below.

Dead	Sleepy	Moderate	Waking Up	Alive

4. Jesus offers the Christians in Sardis clean clothes. This is similar to what the apostle Paul wrote to Christians in Ephesus, encouraging them to "put on Christ." Picture in your mind's eye the Lord coming to you with a clean robe for you. Allow him to dress you up with a coat of righteousness. Now, picture yourself going through your day. How does your spiritual dress affect the way you feel about yourself and your relationship with him?

Pray
Pray that your church may have solid character that is worthy of a godly reputation.

Ask God to give you integrity so that you may be worthy of a godly reputation.

Day 10
Philadelphia: Hold On
Revelation 3:7-13

I believe that trusting in Jesus Christ's death on the cross is the only thing that will get me into heaven. My hard work won't open heaven's door. My theological study won't open heaven's door. Nor will my kindness and compassion to others. All I have to do is believe. Does it not follow that the Christian life is an easy walk from here to heaven?

No. Jesus' words to each of the seven churches call for overcoming dangers from outside and inside the church. Faith is a tenacious, tough determination to love God, discern spiritual dangers, persevere through persecution and keep awake against the enchantments of the world, the flesh and the devil. This is hard. And serious. If we fail, there will be consequences. On the other hand, there will be rewards for those who overcome.

One of the tenets of Reformed theology is the perseverance of the saints. Simply stated, it means that those who truly believe will persevere all the way to heaven. That is what you can see in today's passage. Jesus calls on the Christians in the church of Philadelphia to believe in him so much that they hang on to him in the face of difficult times. That's what we all must continue to do as well.

Approach

It's not easy to give up and trust his power and love instead of our efforts. As you prepare to meet God in his Word, yielding to him in the best thing you can do. Picture yourself collapsing into God's arms. Allow him to hold you for a while, and then write down your thoughts, emotions and impressions.

Study

1. Read Revelation 3:7-13. Fill in the chart with Jesus' message to the church of Philadelphia.

Description of Jesus	
Commendation	
Warning	
Command	
Reward	

2. How would you characterize Jesus' attitude toward this church?

3. Evidently, the church was experiencing denigration by other religious groups. How do Jesus' rewards and challenges meet their needs in verses 9 and 12?

4. How does Jesus' description of himself holding the keys of David address their persecution by the Jews and provide the means of their future entrance into new Jerusalem?

Reflect

1. Jesus' judgment of us takes into account our personal circumstances and abilities. What circumstances are there in your life that affect the way you live?

2. How do you think others would rate your spiritual abilities (gifts and energy to serve God, the gospel and God's people)?

3. How do you think the Lord feels about your use of the spiritual abilities that he has given to you? (This is, of course, a very subjective question. But don't run from it. Ask the Lord what he thinks, and then write down your thoughts and impressions.)

4. Jesus opens a door for the people of Philadelphia, allowing them to enter into the city of God and assume a new identity. The Lord invites you as well into his presence and has made you his son or daughter through your faith in Christ. Sit back and become quiet. Choose to see yourself walking through a door into the presence of God. Allow him to greet you warmly. He then turns and introduces you to the rest of heaven, with your first name followed by his name. It becomes clear to you and everyone else that you are a treasured part of his family. After a while of savoring his favor, write down your thoughts and impressions.

Pray

Thank God for making you a part of his eternal family.

Thank God that he keeps you from tests that are beyond your ability to handle.

Day 11
Laodicea: Repent
Revelation 3:14-22

*T*his church really gets it from the Lord! They were so totally blind that they didn't even know how blind they were. But that is the nature of spiritual blindness. Those who don't think they are blind, are. They can't tell because they have lost their spiritual perception. The only hope for such a spiritual condition is a frontal assault from the Lord and a call to repent.

Of all the seven letters, I believe this one is most appropriate to Christians in America. With all its resources, money, buildings, books and people, the church is overflowing with abundance. Yet our spiritual poverty is obvious. The divorce rate inside the church, the evangelical church, is only a fraction down from the rest of the population. Depression and other mental and emotional problems are as common inside the church as in the population at large. Child abuse inside churches is not much different either. What is going on?

The analysis for the worldliness of the church could go on for pages.

But the remedy need not. We must repent. When we hear the Lord's call to face our sin, we must admit our culpability and be willing to go in another direction. The energy spent shielding ourselves from his presence and soothing our guilty hearts will be freed up to live and serve in divine-human fellowship.

Approach

Each letter ends with the phrase "He who has an ear, let him hear what the Spirit says to the churches." How good are your spiritual ears? Ask the Lord to open up your ears. Sit quietly with a cocked ear and an open heart. Try not to move on to the study until you have a sense of being open to hear and obey. After a time of silence, write down what it's like to have a heart that listens.

Study

1. Read Revelation 3:14-22. Fill in the chart with Jesus' message to the church of Laodicea.

Description of Jesus	
Commendation	
Warning	
Command	
Reward	

2. How would you describe Jesus' attitude toward this church?

3. In your own words, what is this church's problem?

4. In all the other letters Jesus has said he is coming soon. To Laodicea he says, "Here I am." What do you think he means by that?

Reflect

1. Jesus is not impressed with our deeds unless they spring from a warmhearted devotion. Consider your Christian "deeds" over the past several months. Ask the Lord what he thinks about the heart attitudes with which you did them. Sit quietly for a while, and then write down your thoughts and impressions.

2. The Laodiceans are deluded into thinking that they are rich when they are poor. What do you think a spiritually rich church is like?

What do you think a spiritually poor church is like?

How do you rate your church?

3. Each of Jesus' letters has concluded with an admonition to hear. What do you think that Jesus is saying to the church of the present day?

What do you think he is he saying to you?

4. Jesus offers a remedy for the problem of the church of Laodicea: gold refined by fire, white clothes and eye salve. These probably refer to suffering for the truth, righteousness that comes by faith, and the work of the Spirit to open the eyes of the heart. Pause now and ask the Lord for those things for you and your church. Write out your prayer.

Pray
Pray that God would set your church on fire with love for him.

Ask that churches around the world would choose to listen to the Lord's voice.

Day 12
Heavenly Worship
Revelation 19:1-10

*T*oday we change scenes. In chapters 1—3 we read about Jesus' revealing himself to his churches. Each church was encouraged, and five of the seven received warnings. Now Jesus shifts his focus to the world. Chapters 4—18 detail the judgment of earth from the perspective of heaven. Those chapters are fascinating reading. Because they are full of symbolism and parallels, it's not always clear what is going on. We suggest you do your reading with a good commentary in hand.

In this devotional guide we pick up the story line as we come to the other side of the judgments of the earth. God's righteous wrath is almost spent, and all the evil that has been festering in the world for thousands of years is about to be purged. In chapter 19 we get a glimpse of the victory celebration. We are almost on the other side. From the perspective of chapter 19, eternity is just around the corner.

And what will we do when we are safe inside heaven? Worship God.

I hope you have been tasting some of the pleasure of worship as you have been working through these guided quiet times. However great your times have been, they are merely a tantalizing foretaste. I am convinced that there is nothing on earth that will compare with the joy, the peace, the satisfaction, the anticipation, the thrill that is experienced in the worship of our Creator.

Approach

Worship of God brings together our body and soul, our mind and our emotions, ourselves with fellow believers. Sometimes it's reflective and quiet. Sometimes it's spontaneous and noisy. Sometimes it is public, sometimes it is private. However you like to worship God, spend a few minutes doing so now. Try not to move on to the study until you sense that you are in the presence of God. Make a note about your experience.

Study

1. Read Revelation 19:1-10. There is a celebration going on in heaven. We get to look in on a multitude worshiping God. What thoughts and emotions do you experience as you read this passage?

2. Who are those involved in the celebration?

3. What is the message being proclaimed in each song of praise? Fill in the chart on page 56.

	Message	Attitude/Tone
19:1-3		'
19:4		
19:5		
19:6		

4. The hymns in the passage are full of praise to God and reflect the Hallel psalms (113—118). Skim through several of those psalms now and write down your impressions.

Reflect

1. After reading the praise from heaven and earth, join in by writing your own hymn of praise. (Don't feel a need to make it elaborate or poetic. Just express your heart.)

2. Imagine yourself among the multitude offering worship to God at the end of history. What do you think it would be like to be there?

3. Part of the reason for celebration is that the source of evil in the world has finally been judged. How have you personally experienced evil or the effects of injustice or immorality?

What emotions do you experience as you think of God bringing the sources of evil to judgment?

4. Another reason for celebration is the wedding supper of the Lamb. That is, the church finally gets to be with our Lord in heaven. What thoughts come to mind as you think about what it will be like to be finally safe in the covenant of love with Jesus Christ?

Pray
Ask God that those who are suffering from evil may be given patience as he works out his justice.

Ask God to use you and his church to resist injustice until he brings an end to it.

Day 13
Christ the Victor
Revelation 19:11-16

The Messiah was expected to come in as a conquering hero and wipe out the enemies of Israel. Mary, in her delight at becoming the mother of the Christ, exclaimed in Luke 1:51-53:

He has performed mighty deeds with his arm;
  he has scattered those who are proud in their inmost thoughts.
He has brought down rulers from their thrones
  but has lifted up the humble.
He has filled the hungry with good things
  but has sent the rich away empty.

The disciples struggled to understand Jesus throughout his earthly ministry because they were waiting for him to get on his white horse and kick out the Romans. Even after his resurrection the disciples still expected it. In Acts 1:6 they asked, "Lord, are you at this time going to restore the kingdom to Israel?"

What they didn't understand was that the Messiah was coming twice.

As Hebrews 9:28 states it, "Christ was sacrificed once to take away the sins of many people; and he will appear a second time, not to bear sin, but to bring salvation to those who are waiting for him."

Mary's exultation encompassed both comings, the first and the second. What we get to see in today's Scripture is the fulfillment of the Second Coming. This time Christ is coming back as the conquering victor.

Approach

Throughout the letters to the churches, Jesus finished each one with the admonition "He who has an ear to hear, let him hear." Today, before you move on, clear your spiritual ears. Ask God to bring to mind suppressed anger or anxiety that may keep you from hearing. Write down what comes to mind. Ask him to take away anything that would block your ears. Sit for a while cultivating a listening silence.

Study

1. Read Revelation 19:11-16. What names are given to the rider who appears on the white horse (vv. 11, 16)?

2. How does this description compare with those of Jesus in Revelation 1:12-16?

3. From these verses, describe the mission of the white rider.

How does this mission compare with his words to the churches in chapters 1—3?

4. What right does he have to bring judgment on the rest of the world?

Reflect

1. In today's verses we have the beginning of the Second Coming of Christ. Think back over Jesus' ministry in the Gospels. How is his second coming different from his first one?

	First Coming	Second Coming
how he comes		
his appearance		
his use of authority		
other		

2. Jesus' power comes not from the multitudes who follow, or amazing technological weapons, but from the Word of God which comes from his mouth. Look briefly at Genesis 1:1-8. What insight does that give you into the power of God's Word?

3. Although Jesus appears as a victor, he is dressed in a robe dipped in blood. Commentators have several different ideas about where the blood comes from. Some suggest it comes from his enemies. Others suggest that it is the blood of Jesus himself. In 1:5 John describes Jesus as one "who loves us and has freed us from our sins by his blood." I think the second suggestion is closer to the mark. What responses do you have to Jesus as a victorious world ruler who gave his life for the sins of his people?

4. Sitting on a white horse, Jesus has written on his robe *KING OF KINGS AND LORD OF LORDS*. The proper response to Jesus' display in his glory is worship. Spend a few minutes paying him homage. Perhaps you could get down on your knees. Pledge your allegiance to him. Tell him that you will obey him and serve him in any way that he calls you to.

Pray
Ask the Lord for his kingdom to come and his will to be done on earth the way it is done in heaven.

Pray that you would have the strength today to obey him in whatever he calls you to do.

Day 14
The Defeat of Evil
Revelation 19:17—20:3

I love to teach the confirmation class at church. It is made up of fourteen-year-olds who have grown up in the church. When I get to the part about the Second Coming of Christ, their eyes open up with amazement. Most have never thought about it before. When they do, the questions begin to flow.

One of the questions that I hear is, "What happens to the people who don't believe when he returns?"

I use that as an opportunity to talk about faith. In the end, people refuse to believe in Jesus not because the gospel is unbelievable but because it means obedience to God. At the end of history, when Christ returns, unbelievers won't clap their hands for joy, but instead will organize themselves into massive armies of resistance. In today's reading we see a brief description of the battle and the outcome.

Approach
In order to hear the Lord we must be willing to obey and repent when

we discover that we haven't obeyed. Ask God to show you where you are resisting him. As you do this, cultivate a listening attitude. Write down any attitudes or actions of resistance that you discern. Repent of them and ask the Lord to cleanse you. Make a few notes about your responses.

Study

1. Read Revelation 19:17—20:3. How is the "great supper of God" (vv. 17-18) different from the wedding feast of the Lamb in 19:7-8?

How is death involved in both feasts?

2. We are told that the armies of the earth gathered to make war on the rider and his armies (19:19), but we are not given any details of the battle. What do we already know about the battle from 19:15-18 that makes a description of the battle unnecessary?

3. The beast and the false prophet are the subjects of chapters we did not study. (You might want to look at chapter 13.) From these verses today, what do you know about the beast, his prophet and those who have aligned themselves with them?

4. Satan, the source of evil and deception, is treated differently from the rest. Describe what happens to him (20:1-3).

Reflect

1. The battlefield on which the birds feast will not be a pretty sight. How do you respond to the defeat of those who have made themselves active enemies of God?

2. The beast and false prophets represent powerful leaders who were able to deceive people into following them in opposition to God. How did the religious leaders of Jesus' day get people to support them in crucifying Jesus?

3. For what reasons do people today turn away from Christianity to other religions?

4. The beast and the false prophet are punished in the fiery lake of burning sulfur. This seems to indicate a punishment beyond that of others on the battlefield. Why might God have made a distinction between them and others?

5. Satan is bound for a thousand years. Imagine how life on earth might

be different without his presence. Picture going for a walk at midnight anywhere you want to and then leaving your door unlocked after you return. How do you respond?

6. With Satan locked up there will be no active tempter to entice to sin. How might your life be different if you didn't have to cope with temptation?

Pray
Pray that God will give you courage to live in the hope of his coming victory over evil.

Pray that many in the world will turn from resisting God to trusting his Son, Jesus Christ.

Day 15
The Resurrection of the Just
Revelation 20:4-6

One of my favorite areas of the British Museum is on the second floor in the far northeast corner. There you will find, in glass cases, various sizes of mummies surrounded by the objects that were sent with them for the afterlife. As you walk through those rooms, your eyes are drawn back and forth between the huge murals depicting scenes from the Egyptian Book of the Dead and those bodies wrapped in strips of cloth.

In one of my many explorations there I was struck with how "this-worldly" Christianity is in comparison to the other major religions of the world. The Egyptians spent a great deal of thought and energy getting ready to die and live in the world of the spirits. In contrast, the Hebrews were concerned not with the afterlife but with inheriting the land that God had promised to Abraham. When we get to the New Testament, although there is an awareness of the afterlife, it consists not of disembodied spirits but of those who will be resurrected from the dead and raised to live and rule on the earth with Christ.

This world, created by God, is important both now and in the future. I find this Christian understanding of the afterlife appealing. What happens here in the physical is not a mere game that in the end has no meaning. God is the Creator of the world, and he never gives up on it. This is where we will end up.

Approach
Responsiveness to the voice of the Lord requires that we hold loosely to our future plans. Everything we do is subject to his will and open to his revision. How have you responded when the Lord has changed your plans and your hopes were not fulfilled? Write down several incidents.

Give your future goals and plans to him, and sit for a while cultivating an attitude of responsive obedience. After a time of quiet, write down your responses.

Study
1. Read Revelation 20:4-6. What do you learn about death and resurrection from this passage?

2. In what different ways is the authority given to resurrected believers indicated in these verses?

3. What did these souls do to be worthy of their authority? (Read Revelation 13:15-17 for background.)

Reflect

1. Look at verses 4 and 6. It is possible that those who are given authority are only those who were killed for their faith. It is also possible that those who are given authority are not limited to martyrs but are all who have been faithful in Christ. (Read Revelation 1:5-6 and Exodus 19:5-6 for background.) Which way do you think it should be interpreted?

2. The length of their shared authority with Christ is one thousand years—often referred to as the millennium. Some suggest the one-thousand-year reign is symbolic. Others suggest it is literal. What do you think?

What difference will your position make in the way you interpret the passage?

3. Being resurrected with Christ to share the rule of the world with him is a privilege to look forward to! Based on your desires and life experiences, what do you think your contribution to world leadership might be?

4. The testimony to Jesus and the Word of God referred to in today's verses are the powerful means of spiritual ministry. In what ways have you used either one in your life in the past several weeks?

Pray
Ask God to give you the courage and opportunity to speak to someone about (testify to) Jesus soon.

Thank God that he is making you worthy to share authority with Jesus Christ.

Day 16
The Final Rebellion
Revelation 20:7-10

*B*ehind and through the evil that we humans do is a larger spiritual force. Satan took center stage at the beginning of the world in the Garden of Eden. At the end of the world he takes center stage again one last time.

In both situations he uses deception. In the Garden he deceived Eve. In the end he deceives the nations. In the first instance he doesn't challenge God, he merely raises questions about God's good intentions. In the end he incites a flagrant all-out rebellion.

As in the Garden, in the final rebellion the human race shows its colors. Many people give their allegiance to Satan. In the Garden Eve might have sought to justify her behavior by appealing to her innocence. She had never seen the handiwork of the Evil One before; how could she have known where it would lead? In the final rebellion there is no such ᵪcuse. The history of the world displays Satan's handiwork—death and ₃truction for all who succumb to his lies.

What is made plain at the end is merely making explicit what has always been true about sin. It is not that we don't know any better or even that we are ignorant of the consequences. It is that we believe Satan merely because we want to and ignore what it costs.

Approach
God sees us in our sin and temptations. Our best means of dealing with them is to open ourselves up to God and ask him to meet us at the points where we want to sin and hide. Close your eyes and invite the Lord to walk into the recesses of your heart—those dark places where you don't want him to look. After allowing him to be with you there, write down your thoughts and impressions.

Study
1. Read Revelation 20:7-10. After a thousand years, Satan is released. Describe his last efforts on the earth.

2. Gog and Magog, first mentioned in Ezekiel 38—39, symbolize nations that are hostile to God and his people. What does it say about humans that even after a thousand years of Christ's rule on the earth, so many respond to the leadership of Satan?

3. What does it say about Satan that even after a thousand years of Christ's rule he is able to lead a worldwide rebellion?

4. What indications are there that the final efforts of Satan are under God's control and a part of his overall plan?

5. How is Satan's "end" this time different from the preceding one?

Reflect

1. Since the Fall, the human race has been eager to believe Satan's lies about God. What sorts of lies does Satan speak about God that turn us away from him? (Think about this in light of Genesis 3:1-5 as well as your own experience.)

How do you see his lies being spread in our world today?

2. After the Fall it has become "natural" to turn away from God. Until the resurrection, this turning away will be present in believers as well as nonbelievers. Get quiet and examine your own heart. How do you see this allergy to God working in you?

Although our tendency is to resist God, Satan and all our actions are still under God's sovereignty. In what ways can this bring you comfort in the struggles that you face?

Pray

Ask God to give you the power to see through the lies of Satan.

Pray that your family would be delivered from the temptations of the Evil One.

Day 17
The Final Judgment
Revelation 20:11-15

I would like to say that I always obey God out of love and devotion, but it wouldn't be true. I obey God from a variety of motives, one of which is fear. I know that God holds me accountable for my actions, and there will be consequences if I disobey. The book of Proverbs says it this way: "The fear of the Lord is the beginning of wisdom."

I discovered the fear of the Lord in the early days of my Christian walk. I was an insatiable critic. I loved to sneer at people who failed to meet my standards. I remember seeing a guy on my first day of college who must have been the world's all-time nerd. I didn't know the guy and didn't want to. Guess who was assigned to be my roommate.

Then there was the time a student got up in chapel to speak. He didn't do well because he lost his notes. Several weeks later it was my turn to speak in chapel, and sure enough, just before I got up to speak I covered that my notes were gone.

incidences? I don't think so. It began to dawn on me that I was being held accountable for my thoughts and actions. Now when I find haughty thoughts rising in my heart, I am quick to confess and repent.

The framers of the modern world dared to dream about a secular society in which people acted properly just because it was a good idea. After two hundred years, it hasn't worked. Let's face it, we humans need to be held accountable. If there is no God who judges, then there are no moral standards that will hold. Who takes homework seriously if the teacher never looks at it?

The fear of the Lord is the beginning of wisdom for all kinds of reasons, not the least of which is that God won't let our immorality go unpunished. Whether it is the inward movements of a proud heart or the outward actions of lies or murder, God knows and will require an accounting. The judgments exercised by God throughout the course of our lives are mere reflections of the one to be held at the end of history, when the entire human race will stand before God to give an account.

Approach

The presence of God can be both comforting and terrifying. The difference for us is the work of Christ on the cross. Picture yourself at the foot of the cross. Rest awhile in its grace and judgment. Pay attention to your inner responses and jot down a few notes.

Study

1. Read Revelation 20:11-15. What similarities are there between this scene and the preceding one in Revelation 20:7-10?

2. Let's consider the contrasts between this judgment and the preceding one in 20:4-6. How is the throne in this scene different?

What is the difference between what the dead experience in this scene and the preceding judgment?

3. All the dead are raised to judgment. What are the standards by which they are judged?

4. How might the book of life and the book of deeds work together to provide a comprehensive basis for judgment?

5. How can the knowledge that death and the abode of the dead (Hades) are cast into the lake of fire (along with the dead) be a means of hope and eternal confidence?

Reflect
1. The authority and majesty of God are so overwhelming that even the rth and sky flee from his presence. Imagine yourself before God on his

throne with no backdrop to distract—all you see is God. How do you respond?

2. Picture a vast space in which all the dead of the ages are standing before God to give account of their lives. If you were allowed to listen in, what might they be saying to justify themselves?

3. Look at Colossians 1:21-23 and 2:13-17. Based on these verses, what should/will you say when you stand before God to give account?

Pray
Thank God that he has provided Christ, rather than our own works, as the means by which we can be judged.

Pray that God would raise up many who can share the gospel with those who don't yet have their names written in the book of life.

Day 18
The New Jerusalem
Revelation 21:1-4

"There are no cats in America," sang the mice in *An American Tail*. The animated cartoon about immigration to America pictured a land with limitless abundance and opportunities. However, the idealistic mice found shortly after their arrival, much to their pain and dismay, that there *are* cats in America.

It doesn't matter where you go. This side of heaven there is always something wrong, something that doesn't fit right. People from many Two-Thirds World countries long for a chance to get in on political freedom and economic opportunities in the Western world.

Personally, I couldn't wait to get out of America. Being an aspiring flower child of the sixties, the rampant materialism and individualism of the U.S. culture made me sick. I looked for someplace else to take my family, and we ended up in England. We loved our two years there. And we did escape American materialism and individualism. However, we discovered a resistance to innovation, a fear of change and a suspicion of emotional intimacy that left us feeling out of place.

Where can we go to satisfy the longing we all feel? Some turn to nostalgia, thinking things must have been better in times past. Some of us look to the future, when human progress is supposed to take us to new levels of technological and human development. We are, as the writer of Hebrews states, longing for a better country, looking forward to the city with foundations whose architect and builder is God. Today in your quiet time you get to read about what it is like to get into that place.

Approach

What longings do you have that are unfulfilled? Ask God not to take away your longings but increase them so you may anticipate their fulfillment in God's new world.

Study

1. Read Revelation 21:1-4. Describe the scene that is unfolding before John's eyes.

2. Compare the new heaven and earth to the cursed earth in Genesis 3:16-24. How are they different? Fill in the chart.

Cursed Earth	New Heaven and Earth

3. What words and phrases tell us what our relationship to God will be like in the new heaven and earth?

4. The new city is dressed as a bride; it symbolizes the marriage between God and his people. How will our relationship to God in the new heaven and earth be like a marriage?

Reflect
1. Everything is to be made new. If you could have your life made over again, how would it be different? What would you keep?

What would you change?

2. The new Jerusalem is described as a bride beautifully dressed for her husband just prior to the wedding ceremony. Imagine that you are within hours of entering into a marriage to God. What emotions does the anticipation create in you?

3. Every source of pain and sorrow will be banished in the new heaven

and earth. What painful events have you experienced in the past several months?

What were/are your feelings?

How did you act?

Are there any lingering effects?

How can the knowledge of what is to come give you the resources you need for today?

Pray
Thank God that he will give you a new life and a fresh start.

Ask God to give you the growing conviction and strength that the hope of heaven provides.

Pray for several people you know who are in pain. Ask God to give them a new hope of his coming new world.

Day 19
Divine Citizenship
Revelation 21:5-8

Take a trip to another country and you will understand elements of citizenship that you never considered. When you get off the airplane, you go through customs and immigration. While thumbing suspiciously through your passport, the immigration official grills you about why you have come and how long you plan to stay. Once you get past the official, you get to pick up your luggage and stand in another line where your bags are opened to make sure you aren't bringing in anything they don't want. Occasionally, someone gets turned away. The whole experience, whether you get turned away or not, communicates that you don't belong there.

How different when you return to your own country. While foreigners stand in line, you get to zip through as the officials take a cursory look at your passport. A few will even offer a smile and "welcome home" sorts of greetings. You know that you belong. This is your place.

One day God's people are going to make it to the new Jerusalem.

When we arrive, we will be welcomed with smiles and greetings of "Welcome home." The privileges of citizenship there will be enhanced because, as we know, only citizens get in.

Approach
God is the center of our lives. But sometimes there are so many things around us that we can't see him. Picture God as the center of a wagon wheel. Perhaps you could even draw one in the space below. One by one, connect each spoke of your busy life to him. After you have done that, you can allow your life to roll forward in an orderly way. What is your response?

Study
1. Read Revelation 21:5-8. What do you think God means by "It is done"?

by "I am . . . the Beginning and the End"?

2. The water of life is given without cost, but there are conditions. What are they?

3. The person who "overcomes" will inherit all this and will be God's

son or daughter. What do you think *overcome* means?

4. How do the contrasting images of "spring of the water of life" and "fiery lake of burning sulfur" help us understand the coming future?

Reflect

1. In the new city, those who thirst are promised the water of life. Likewise, Jesus promised that those who hunger and thirst for righteousness will be filled. From your own experience, how do you describe a hunger and thirst for God?

2. We don't have to wait until the new heaven and earth to experience the quenching of spiritual thirst. Jesus said, "If anyone is thirsty, let him come to me and drink. Whoever believes in me, as the Scripture has said, streams of living water will flow from within him" (Jn 7:37-38). How have you experienced the living water of Jesus?

3. Spiritual desire is both satisfying and enticing. Jonathan Edwards wrote, "Spiritual good is of a satisfying nature. . . . And the more a man experiences this . . . satisfying sweetness, the more earnestly will he hunger and thirst for more." Likewise, Bernard of Clairvaux wrote, "We taste Thee, O Thou Living Bread / And long to feast upon Thee still; / We drink of Thee, the Fountainhead / And thirst our souls from Thee to fill."

Sit in silence and allow yourself to reach out to God for more of his loving care.

Pray

Ask God to increase your spiritual hunger.

Pray that your church would be a place where people are both spiritually fed and increasingly hungry.

Day 20
The Shape of the City
Revelation 21:9-21

W hen in England, I was shocked to find how powerful the cathedrals were in calling me to worship. I went as a tourist to look at the monuments to the faith of ages past. What I discovered were sermons in stone that still spoke.

Inside and outside I was surrounded with meaning. As I walked toward a cathedral from the parking lot, the spires and steeple pointed me upward toward God. The high arched entryway stood as a portal welcoming me to worship. Once inside, the height of the ceilings and the arched supports lifted my eyes heavenward. The aisles laid out in the shape of the cross called me to face my sin. The stained-glass windows in rich colors and skillfully rendered figures called me to emulate the men and women of faith who have gone before. The altar paintings and embroidered cloth drops played off the windows and challenged me to look for and think about the presence of God. Everywhere I looked, I could sense that there was more meaning than I could see. I made it a practice to look for the volunteer guides who were always on duty and to ask lots of questions.

Each time I went in I was filled with a sense of reverence and awe. I knew that God had been worshiped continually for hundreds of years inside this special building, and I was invited to join in. Surrounded by that sense of history and piety, I experienced a refreshing clarity of mind and cleansing of soul. I felt exhilarated and clean from the inside out. While other tourists walked by, I often felt an urge to drop to my knees and pray.

With that experience in mind, I am eager to take my place in the new Jerusalem. How great it will be to live in a city that is designed for those who want to live continually in the presence of the living God! A living sermon in design and materials will surround us, symbols that call us to live an eternal life of worship. The cleansing exhilaration of those English cathedrals is only a meager foretaste of what is to come.

Approach

What place draws you to worship God? The sanctuary of your church? Perhaps a stream in a nearby park? I love to walk by the Gulf of Mexico and pray. If you cannot get to your favorite spot now, place yourself there in your mind's eye. Allow yourself to be drawn to God, and sit awhile in an attitude of worship. After a time of worship, jot down your reflections.

Study

1. Read Revelation 21:9-21. Stand with John and the angel on the mountain. Describe what you see.

2. What clues are we given to help us see that the new Jerusalem is a symbol for the people of God?

3. John sees twelve gates with the names of the twelve tribes of Israel inscribed on them. How has the nation of Israel functioned as a gate for the people of God?

How have the apostles functioned as the foundations?

4. We are given a detailed description of the city's dimensions as well as the jewels with which it is built. In what ways can these descriptions help us think about the future condition of God's people?

Reflect
1. The gates of the city are the tribes of Israel. The Scriptures of the Old Testament, the writings of Israel, have made it possible for millions to grow spiritually. Which part of the Old Testament is your favorite?

How has it helped you to enter into a deeper relationship with God?

2. The apostles are the foundations of the city walls. Their experiences with Jesus Christ, recorded in the Gospels, and their instructions for Christian living, recorded in the Epistles, have also contributed to the guidance of the church. Which part of the New Testament is your favorite?

How have the writings of the apostles and the first followers of Jesus contributed to your growing relationship with God?

3. How does John's vision give you encouragement for your Christian walk?

Pray
Ask God to give a vision of the church's future glory to your Christian leaders as they work through the day-to-day issues of Christian ministry.

Thank God for the godly people who, while living generations ago, have contributed to your spiritual growth.

Day 21
The Light of the City
Revelation 21:22-27

Dorothy, the Lion, the Scarecrow, the Tin Man and Toto followed the yellow brick road to the Emerald City of Oz. Although they were impressed by its splendor, they wanted to see the Great Oz. It was from the wizard of Oz, not the city in all its glory, that they hoped to get a means to go back to Kansas.

In our culture we often confuse the outward with the inward. Doctors fix the body but don't know much about the soul. Our scientists study the material makeup of the world from molecules to galaxies, but we lack a way to think about its Creator. What is the source and center of life? Is there a purpose, a meaning, a Being behind it all? Dorothy and company would never have gotten back to Kansas if they had spent their time observing the city and looking for answers in its composition.

I wrote in yesterday's introduction about how much I delighted in visiting cathedrals because of the way they drew me into worship. But there is another side to the story. Although most of those I visited in

England, like Salisbury, Canterbury and Worcester, were active places of worship, there were a few in other parts of Europe that were merely museums. Run by the state or some charitable foundation, they were testimonies to the faith of ages past and were now only shells. No one worshiped there anymore. They were beautiful, but dead.

The reason for the cathedral is not found in its design or its craftsmanship, but in the One whom it was designed to honor. Likewise, the reason for the world is found in the One to whom it points. And so it is with the new Jerusalem. One day we will live in a place whose structure and splendor will continually point us to the presence of God.

Approach

The presence of God is behind everything that we do. Only by the eyes of faith can we discern him. Think through your actions and activities for this past week. Write them down. Prayerfully consider your list, and ask God to show you ways that he is with you and working in your life.

Study

1. Read Revelation 21:22-27. Describe what it is like inside the city.

2. The image of light in the Scriptures frequently symbolizes moral purity. What indications are there that this is what it stands for in the new Jerusalem as well?

3. What are the worldwide effects of the presence of God dwelling among his people?

4. We are told that entrance to the city is limited to those whose names are recorded in the Lamb's book of life. What does the Lamb's book of life stand for, and how can you get your name in it?

Reflect

1. Read Genesis 1:3, 14. Note that when God first created the world, he made light before he made the physical sources of light. Now at the new creation he again provides light without its physical sources. Meditate on light as a symbol of God's presence. Close your eyes and imagine yourself in a world without physical light. What would it be like? Consider what problems you might encounter and how you would respond. How do you think you might feel? What do you think you might fear?

As the darkness is replaced by a bright light, how do you respond?

2. Jesus told the disciples that they were to be lights of the world. How have fellow Christians functioned as a light in your life?

3. Have you ever been robbed or had something of yours stolen? (Perhaps you haven't, but someone close to you has.) How did it make you feel?

How has it affected the way you live?

Imagine yourself now in the new Jerusalem, where there is no need for locked doors. How do you respond?

Pray
Ask God to make your church a place where the coming light of the new Jerusalem can be glimpsed today.

Pray that the Lord would make you a means of light to your family and friends.

Day 22
The Center of the City
Revelation 22:1-5

I love to travel. I'm not much of an outdoors sort of person, but I am attracted to cities. Places like New York, San Francisco, Chicago, Paris and London conjure up a mystic sense of anticipation. I've read about them, seen glimpses of them in movies, and I can't wait to see them for myself.

When I visit American cities, I usually have two first impressions. First, they all look the same: the same strips of fast-food restaurants in the suburbs and the same sorts of tall buildings in the business districts. My other response is a sense of incompleteness. I come away with a sense that the cities have no soul, no center. You can drive up one street and down another, you can look up at the tall buildings, but when do you arrive at the heart of the city? I almost feel like nobody is home. In contrast, cities of a hundred years ago had a city square made up of a courthouse, a church and a public gathering place.

The new Jerusalem has a center—the throne of God and the Lamb.

When we walk down the streets of God's new community, there will be a source to which we are drawn and from which flows the water of life. We will find somebody at home, and we will be home.

Approach
Where do you feel at home? Is it the place you live now, or do you recall with fondness another time and another place? God wants us to feel at home with him. Imagine yourself in that place where you find comfort, safety and belonging. Invite God to be with you there. Relax in his presence and enjoy being at home with him. Write down your thoughts and impressions.

Study
1. Read Revelation 22:1-5. The source of life and the center of the city is the throne of God and the Lamb. From these verses describe that relationship between God and his redeemed community.

2. What different elements of the new community are mentioned that make it a healthy place to live in?

3. The tree of life first mentioned in Genesis 3:21-24 now reappears. What is the tree of life like?

Why do you think God allows the human race access to it now, when it had been forbidden?

4. Look over Genesis 2:1-8. Besides the tree, how else might life in the new heaven and earth be like life in the Garden of Eden?

Reflect
1. The water of life flows down the middle of the city and is bridged by the tree of life. This is a great image of refreshment and nurture. Water quenches our thirst and cleanses our bodies. We don't have to wait until we get to the new Jerusalem to benefit from God's water of life.

Picture yourself by a fresh flowing stream of clear water. Place yourself on a flat rock beside the stream. Take your shoes off and allow the water to run over your feet. Climb down in the water and let it flow over your legs and up to your waist. Lie back in the water and allow it to flow over you and inside you, cleansing your heart and satisfying your thirst. Write down your thoughts and impressions.

2. The tree of life is so fruitful that it bears each month rather than once a year. In Isaiah the Lord invites us to his spiritual banquet: "Come, buy wine and milk without money and without cost. Why spend money on what is not bread, and your labor on what does not satisfy? Listen, listen

to me, and eat what is good, and your soul will delight in the richest of fare" (Is 55:1-2).

Ask the Lord to feed you now. Perhaps you could use the background of the Twenty-third Psalm, where the Lord sets a table before David in a quiet pasture beside a stream. Enjoy a meal with him. Listen to what he might be calling you to do, and receive with gratitude what he is providing for you. Write down your responses.

3. In the new community there will be constant light that comes from the Lord's presence. That too we can enjoy now. Allow the Lord's light and love to shine down on you. Picture yourself on a beach, or perhaps sitting beside that stream on the rock. Feel his warmth shine down on you. Allow him to expose the dark places in your heart and take away anything that would not be pleasing to him. Make a note of your responses.

Pray
Ask God to feed the members of your congregation with his Spirit and Word.

Thank God for the ways that he continues to feed you and provide you with spiritual healing for your pains and hurts.

Day 23
Word of the Future
Revelation 22:6-11

*H*istorically, prophets have had a rough time. For one thing, it seems like people always confuse the message with the messenger. Elijah declared God's message of a drought in judgment for Ahab's sins. Ahab got mad, not at God but at Elijah. Elijah spent several years running for his life. When Elijah finally came out of hiding, Ahab greeted him: "Is that you, you troubler of Israel?"

Although prophets were a pain, they were important to have around. Their close connection with God and potential knowledge of the future might provide important bits of information or influence that could improve the nation's military, political or economic prospects. The same King Ahab who felt God's judgment through Elijah benefited when another prophet told him about impending attacks by a hostile nation.

Another problem related to prophets was that of verification. Since the prophet spoke about the future, it was hard to know if what he said was true. What if Ahab prepared for war with the wrong nation? What if the prophet foretold success in a battle, and it turned out to be a loss?

The Old Testament standard for verification was fulfillment. You could tell the prophecy was true when it happened. In the meantime, the king had to take a risk in deciding whether to act on or ignore the prophet's message.

As with prophecies from the Old Testament, many people who have read the book of Revelation felt it to be a pain—all those strange images and all that talk about judgment and eternal death. Martin Luther wasn't even sure that the book of Revelation should have been included in the Scripture. On the other hand, the promise of a new heaven and earth in which sin and pain are removed sounds attractive. Maybe it's true after all. Another problem with Revelation is that of verification: how do we know that what John says is true? If we use the standard of the Old Testament, we won't know until it happens. In the meantime, we have a choice to make. Do we risk believing it or don't we?

Approach

Listening to God is risky. How do we know that we are hearing from God or merely from our own hearts? It's a risk of faith, and those who listen may get it wrong. But those who don't listen never hear. Ask God to give you discernment between your own thoughts and his voice, and then spend some time in quiet, cultivating a listening heart. Write down your thoughts and impressions.

Study

1. Read Revelation 22:6-11. From both this passage and the rest of Revelation, what answer would you give to the question "Why should I trust that the book of Revelation is true?"

2. Twice in these verses the word *soon* is used for the events of Revelation and Jesus' return. What do you think *soon* means in the context of Revelation?

How does the impending nature of the events affect the way you respond to Revelation's teaching?

3. John is told to make sure that the events he has been shown are told to others. From what the angel says in verse 11, it doesn't appear that he expects John's telling to change anyone's behavior. Why then should the message be made known?

4. The angel refuses John's mistaken attempt to worship him instead of God. What does his response indicate about John, angels and all who believe?

Reflect

1. As there was at the beginning of chapter 1, there is a blessing offered for those who believe and obey the words of Revelation. As we come to the end of the book, consider: how have you been affected by your time in Revelation?

How has it affected your vision of Jesus Christ?

How has it affected your attitude toward the church?

How has it affected your attitude toward the future?

How has it affected the way you live day by day?

2. The angel tells John, "Worship God!" How have the rich pictures of worship in Revelation affected your own worship of God?

3. Spend some time now in worship. To help you, turn back to 1:12-18 and the first vision of Jesus that John sees. Read it over slowly. Fix those images in your mind. Spend time in praise and thanksgiving. Write down your responses.

Pray
Pray that the message of Jesus' return would take on new importance and power among believers.

Ask the Lord to increase your sense of hope and anticipation of the Lord's coming.

Pray that those in your family who have not yet believed in the Lord would do so soon.

Day 24
The Imminent Expectation
Revelation 22:12-17

J esus Christ is coming back soon. The first generation of the church thought that they were the last, that Jesus was coming for them. Many in each generation since then, based on the words of Jesus himself, thought the same. Martin Luther was sure that the pope was the antichrist and that the events of Revelation were unfolding in the sixteenth century. In nineteenth-century America there were groups that sold all their property and went up on a hill to wait for the Lord. Not too long ago, a book that dated Jesus' return in 1986 sold millions . . . before 1986!

Well, is he or isn't he coming back soon? Was each generation mistaken to believe that it would happen during their watch? Evidently God counts time differently from the way we do. *Soon* to him means something different from what it does to us. After all, what's a couple of thousand years if you live for eternity? When you are dealing with God, you have to take time on his terms, not ours.

The Lord wants us to live on the razor's edge of expectation. It's just fine with him if each generation thinks it is the last. The sense of expectation of his imminent return is important for our spiritual health. For one thing, it keeps us accountable. He doesn't leave us a lot of time to mess around and then clean up our action at the end. We need to keep our spiritual accounts up to date. Second, the sense of imminent expectation strengthens our hope. It's hard to invest in something when results may not come in for a thousand years or so. But when you know that what you are looking forward to could come in a couple of years, or at least in your lifetime, that sounds better.

Approach
Since the Lord wants us to live in expectation, wait for the Lord this morning. Lay your needs, struggles and concerns before him to see what he will say and do. Write them out in the space below. Then wait for a while; sit as long as you can. After waiting, write down how the exercise affected your attitude toward your problems and your relationship to the Lord.

Study
1. Read Revelation 22:12-17. The book of Revelation began with a vision of Jesus' identity; it also closes with affirmations of who he is. What does Jesus want us to know about who he is?

2. How do Jesus' statements about himself imply that he is the fulfillment of Scripture (v. 16)?

3. Why do you think there have been so many affirmations about who Jesus is in Revelation?

4. How do the statements about who Jesus is affect you?

5. Jesus' coming has consequences for everybody. What is his standard of judgment?

6. There is a firm warning of exclusion from eternity in these verses. From verses 14-15, who are those who are "inside" and those on the "outside"?

7. Verse 17 in an invitation. Describe the attitude of the invitation and who extends it.

What light does the invitation put on the warning in verse 15?

Reflect
1. Jesus says that he will reward each person according to what he or she has done. How does that square with the teaching in the rest of the New

Testament that only those who have faith in Jesus' cross will be qualified for heaven? For example, look at James 2:14-26 and Romans 3:19-24. How can the two themes of faith and deeds be reconciled?

2. In verse 12 Jesus says that he is bringing his reward with him. When have you been motivated by a reward?

How do you respond to the idea that Jesus is coming with a reward for you?

3. Verse 17 includes both desire and invitation. Consider: what sort of invitation do you sense being extended to you from God? Sit quietly for a while and listen. Then see if you can put your sense of the invitation into words.

Hearing God's invitation stirs up within us a hunger for him. How would you rate your desire for him?

Weak	Moderate	Strong

Ask God to increase your hunger, and then sit for a while in expectation. Write down how your heart is responding.

4. Those who hear the invitation join in the call and invite others to come as well. To whom would you like to extend the invitation?

Pray

Pray for several of your friends or family members who have not yet responded to the Lord's call.

Ask God to increase your sense of direction for the deeds he has for you to do and for which he will reward you.

Ask God to help you grow in trusting his grace for your salvation.

Day 25
Pay Attention
Revelation 22:18-21

*T*he church of Jesus Christ has a mission and a message. If the church gives up its message and mission, it no longer has a reason to exist. It becomes merely a relic of history, like those cathedrals that are now state-owned museums. Or like an old car in a junkyard whose engine no longer works, the church without its message and mission ends up unable to move and becomes a rusty heap in a junkyard. The mission and the message is that we are to witness to Jesus Christ, who is the Lord of heaven and earth and who is the means by which all are judged.

There are pressures, subtle and overt, that seek to dilute, discount and distort what we believe and what we proclaim. The overt resistance comes from those who deny Jesus Christ is Lord or who choose to believe in Islam, Buddhism or some other religion. To accommodate them we are tempted to say that Jesus is just one way to God and every other way is OK too.

The subtle pressures come from the unspoken relativistic assumptions of our culture. It is assumed throughout our educational experience that it is not possible to know truth about God or moral standards of conduct. Since these things can't be known, it is wrong to believe that someone could be condemned for what they believe or how they act. We Christians are tempted to say that all that really matters is that people be sincere and loving.

While both pressures, the overt and the subtle, are serious, I believe that the subtle pressures are the most dangerous and difficult. As we call others to believe and obey Jesus Christ, we may find that our words sound weak and hollow. How can we respond to these pressures? First, we should not be surprised. Just as it is inevitable that water and air cause rust on metal, so it is inevitable that the assumptions of our culture will wear away at our souls. So second, we need to submit to constant maintenance. Just as sandpaper and repair keep our metallic contraptions in working order, so the sandpaper of the Lord and his work inside us keep us alive. In this process God's Word is both the sandpaper of judgment by which we are cleansed and the spirit of truth by which we are renewed.

Approach

Learning to listen to the Lord allows us to discern the voice of the Spirit, recognize the voice of the world and sort out our own thoughts and desires. Get quiet and open up your spiritual ears. See if you can untwist what these voices may be saying inside your heart and mind.

The World	Our Thoughts and Desires	The Holy Spirit

Study

1. Read Revelation 22:18-21. What warnings are given as we come to the conclusion of Revelation?

Why do you think such warnings are necessary?

2. Compare the warning at the end of the book with the promise at the beginning (1:3). Together, what do they say about the book of Revelation?

Reflect

1. By its nature, Revelation seems to encourage speculation. However, in light of the closing warning, we must handle it with care. What do you think would constitute taking away from the message of the book?

What would constitute adding to it?

2. Some commentators feel that it is more than a mere coincidence that the book of Revelation ends with this warning. They suggest that the warning relates not only to Revelation but to the entire Bible. What are ways that people take away from the Bible?

How do people add to it?

3. The blessing of the Lord's grace is extended to his people in the closing benediction. This should bring to mind again just how much Jesus loves his church. Think back on Jesus' letters to the churches in the first half of this guide. What did you learn about the way the Lord expresses his love to his people?

4. Consider the second half of the guide, which began with chapter 19. What did you learn about God's care and plans for his people?

5. How will these guided quiet times affect your attitude toward the church?

6. The central theme of Revelation is that Jesus Christ is coming back soon. What have you learned about the return of Christ from your guided quiet times in Revelation?

7. The return of Christ is to be a present and motivating desire on the part of his people. What place does the knowledge of Christ's return have in your day-to-day life?

Here is a challenging standard that fits in with the spirit of Revelation. As Christians, if we want anything more than we want the return of Jesus Christ, then our priorities are wrong. If you are like me, you must repent frequently and move Christ's return back up on your list of priorities. It is always being replaced by hundreds of other things. As you finish this book, join me in repenting again and lifting up your eyes to look for our Lord Jesus Christ to return. "Amen. Come, Lord Jesus."

Pray

Pray that God's people throughout the world would do ministry and mission in the light of the Lord's return.

Pray that those in your family who don't yet believe would do so before he returns.

Pray that Jesus Christ would come back soon.